# Finding the Way Home

# Finding the Way Home

Poems of Awakening & Transformation

Edited by
## Dennis Maloney

WHITE PINE PRESS / BUFFALO, NEW YORK

ACKNOWLEDGMENTS begin on page 184.

The publication of this book has been made possible with public funds from the New York State Council on the Arts, a State Agency.

First Edition

Library of Congress Control Number: 2009937821

ISBN: 978-1-935210-12-2

Printed and bound in the United States of America.

White Pine Press
P.O. Box 236
Buffalo, NY 14201
www.whitepine.org

# Table of Contents

## ALONG THE SILK ROAD:
## POEMS FROM INDIA & THE MIDDLE EAST

## I AM NOT EMPTY, I AM OPEN: POEMS FROM EUROPE

## Afterword

# INTRODUCTION

Good poetry contains the kind of knowledge we search for, the kind which resonates in the heart as well as in the mind. The poems in this anthology are timeless, span two milennia, and are drawn from many centuries and cultures. What they share is a living spirit that can help us change the way we see ourselves and the world. As Swedish poet Tomas Transtromer says in his poem about the painter Vermeer, " I am not empty, I am open." A good poem may open a door or window we didn't know existed.

In this age of the twenty-four/seven media assault from all directions, good poetry has the capacity to  slow us down, make us listen and pay attention. For the general reader this book gathers a unique selection of direct and accessible poetry that can awaken and transform. For the poet, it is perhaps a source book from which to draw inspiration. The great Japanese poet Basho referred to his practice as Kado, the way of poetry. He thought of poetry as a way of life and a source of enlightenment. He also suggested that as poets we "don't follow in the footsteps of the masters but seek what they sought." Or as the Japanese zen poet Ryokan says in one of his poems

> It is fine to see young people
> stay home and enthusiastically compose poems,
> imitating the classic styles of the Han and Wei

and mastering the contemporary styles of the
     Tang.
Although their style is excellent, even novel,
unless the poem says something from the inner
     heart
what shall we do with so many empty words?

The teacher Joseph Cambell often spoke of the hero's journey or leaving the world of social achievment to seek the inner power and harmony that is often missing in life. He lamented the fact that comtemporary society no longer offered an appropriate ritual system to bring the world of nature together with our own inner nature. He suggested that where ever there is a way or path, it is someone else's footprint and that, as the Spanish poet Antonio Machado suggests, each of us must find his or her own way:

Traveler, your footprints
are the only road, nothing else.
Traveler, there is no road;
you make your own path as you walk.
As you walk, you make your own road,
and when you look back
you see the path
you will never travel again.
Traveler, there is no road;
only a ship's wake on the sea.

May the poems in this collection set you off on your own adventures.

Dennis Maloney
— Big Sur, California

## A Note on the Selection of the Poems

The bulk of the poems in this anthology are drawn from books published by White Pine Press over the past thirty-seven years. During that time we have attracted a family of poets whose voices range from ancient China and India to contemporary America and Europe. In addition, I have included the work of a few poets whose poems I admire but because of varied circumstances we have not yet published in book form.

Many of the original books from which the poems are drawn are in print and available at our website, whitepine.org.

# THE WAY TO COLD MOUNTAIN

# MOUNTAIN

# Poems from China

Looking for a place to settle out
Cold Mountain will do it
fine wind among thick pines
the closer you listen the better the sound
under them a man  his hair turning white
mumbling mumbling Taoist texts
he's been here ten years unable to return
completely forgotten the way by which he came

—Han Shan
*Translated by Art Tobias*


People ask the way to Cold Mountain
Cold Mountain  the road doesn't go through
by summer the ice still hasn't melted
Sunrise is a blur beyond the fog
imitating me  how can you get here
if your heart was like mine
you'd return to the very center

—Han Shan
*Translated by Art Tobias*

If you're always silent and say nothing
what stories will the younger generation have to tell
if you hide yourself away in the thickest woods
how will your wisdom's light shine through
a bag of bones is not a sturdy vessel
the wind and frost do their work soon enough
plow a stone field with a clay ox
and the harvest day will never come

—Han Shan
*Translated by Art Tobias*


Me   I'm happy with the everyday way
like the mist and vines in these rockstrewn ravines
this wilderness is so free and vast
my old friends   the white clouds   drift idly off
there is a road   but it doesn't reach the world
mindless   who can be disturbed by thoughts
at night I sit alone on a stone bed
while the round moon climbs the face of Cold Mountain

—Han Shan
*Translated by Art Tobias*

I laugh at myself, old man, with no strength left
inclined to piney peaks, in love with lonely paths
oh well, I've wandered down the years to now
free in the flow; and floated home the same
                a drifting boat

—Shih-Te
*Translated by Jerome Seaton*

not going, not coming
rooted, deep and still
not reaching out, not reaching in
just resting, at the center
a single jewel, the flawless crystal drop
in the blaze of its brilliance
the way beyond

—Shih-Te
*Translated by Jerome Seaton*

# RETURNING ALONE

under a declining sun, as cicadas cry
I return alone to the temple in the woods
whose rough pine doors are never pulled shut
the slivered moon edging along beside me.

grassy forms crystallize amidst mist-shrouded forces
the scent of blossoms saturated the air with pungent mystery.

now and then I hear dogs barking,
once again press my way between green creepers

—Shou Ch'uan
*Translated by Jerome Seaton*

## END OF THE ROAD

here I am, seventy-six
a life's worth of karma just about gone.
alive, I don't lust for Heaven;
dead, I won't worry about Hell.
I'll loose my grip and lie down beyond the world
given in to fate, freely, without constraint.

—Tao K'ai
*Translated by Jerome Seaton*

## POET'S ZEN

no hiding the pain I feel as twilight darkens
incense from India may not be ritual enough.
every day, after chanting the Heart three times,
I give in, again, to the seductions of poet's Zen.

—Ta Hsiang
*Translated by Jerome Seaton*

the human body is a little universe
its chill tears, so much windblown sleet
beneath our skins, mountains bulge, brooks flow,
within our chests lurk lost cities, hidden tribes.

wisdom quarters itself in our tiny hearts.
liver and gall peer out, scrutinize a thousand miles.
follow the path back to its source, or else be
a house vacant save for swallows in the eaves.

—Shih Shu
*Translated by Jerome Seaton*

## JUST DONE

A month alone behind closed doors
forgotten books, remembered, clear again.
Poems come, like water to the pool
Welling,

                up and out,
from perfect silence.

—Yuan Mei
*Translated by Jerome Seaton*

## ZAZEN ON THE MOUNTAIN

The birds have vanished down the sky.
Now the last cloud drains away.

We sit together, the mountain and me,
until only the mountain remains.

—Li Bai
*Translated by Sam Hamill*

# I MAKE MY HOME IN THE MOUNTAINS

You ask why I live
alone in the mountain forest,

and I smile and am silent
until even my soul grows quiet:

it lives in the other world,
one that no one owns.

The peach trees blossom.
The water continues to flow.

—Li Bai
*Translated by Sam Hamill*

# DRINKING ALONE BENEATH THE MOON

One jar of wine among the flowers,
no dear friend to drink with:
I offer a cup to the moon.
With my shadow there are three of us,
but the moon doesn't know how to drink,
and my shadow can't help but follow me.
Still, I'll make do with their company,
have fun and make the most of spring.
I sing and the moon rolls around,
I dance and my shadow leaps about.
While I'm lively we enjoy each other,
when I get too drunk we go our own ways.
Let's keep this undemanding friendship
till we join together in the far Cloud River.

—Li Bai
*Translated by David Lunde*

# DREAMING OF LI BAI (I)

Parting with the dead, one eventually stops sobbing,
but when parting with the living sorrow never ends.
You're exiled to Yelang in Jiangnan, place plagued by
malaria,
and no news of you, old friend. But you enter my dream
tonight for you are always in my thoughts.
You are now tangled up in the nets of the law;
how did you free your wings to fly here?
It makes me fear this soul of yours is not of one still liv-
ing.
The road between us is too long to measure.
When your soul came this way, you could see green
maples,
but journeying back it will travel through dark passes.
As I wake, the sinking moon floods the roof-beams with
light,
and I stare about, half-expecting it will shine on your face.
Between us the water is deep and the waves broad and
tall—
don't let the water-dragons seize you, my friend!

—Du Fu
*Translated by David Lunde*

# WRITTEN WHILE TRAVELING AT NIGHT

Sparse grass, a faint wind along the shore,
the tall mast of my solitary boat in the night,
stars hanging low over the flat, wide plains,
moon bobbing up from the great river's waves...
How can a man make a name by writing?
Old age and illness have ended my career.
Drifting, drifting...what am I like?
Between heaven and earth, a wind-blown gull.

—Du Fu
*Translated by David Lunde*

# THE WINE OF ENDLESS LIFE

a body without business
a mind that knows no suffering
a whole life spent upon the shores
of stormy seas.
don't seek favor
don't clamber after fame
accomplishment and glory
giving up and getting, are empty
both the same
this floating life is petals falling
emptied past the eye
serving the state
       is a dream
serving yourself
       is the same.

—Ch'en Ts'ao-an
*Translated by Jerome P. Seaton*

## ON THE STREAM, AGAIN

A just stopped bell
over the grass blue air—

small flame
burns in fading haze;

the old year's stream
returns in the canyon,

and in night's chill
wide armed sky falls frost;

all man's life
but an insect's knee,

and all the world's paths
bent as sheep's-gut;

in old age
I've forgot the fine rules;

only wild song
prolongs the recall.

—Lu Yu
*Translated by David Gordon*

# WRITTEN ON A COLD EVENING

The poet must work with brush and paper,
but this is not what makes the poem.
A man doesn't go in search of a poem—
the poem comes in search of him.

—Yang Wan-Li
*Translated by Jonathan Chaves*

# EVENING: SITTING IN THE WO-CHIH STUDIO

The room is stuffy and uncomfortable:
I open a window to let in the cool air.
Forest trees shade the sunlight;
the inkstone on my desk glitters jade green.
My hand reaches naturally for a book of poetry
and I read some poems out loud.

The ancients had a mountain of sorrows
but my heart is a calm as a river.
If I am different from them,
how is it that they move me so deeply?

The feeling passes and I laugh to myself.
Outside a cicada urges on the sunset.

—Yang Wan-Li
*Translated by Jonathan Chaves*

# ON RECEIVING MY LETTER OF TERMINATION

The time has come to devote myself to my hiker's stick;
I must have been a Buddhist monk in a former life!
Sick, I see returning home as kind of pardon.
A stranger here—being fired is like being promoted.
In my cup, thick wine; I get crazy-drunk,
eat my fill, then stagger up the green mountain.
The southern sect, the northern sect, I've tried them all:
this hermit has his own school of Zen philosophy.

—Yuan Hung-tao
*Translated by Jonathan Chaves*

# BREAK THE MIRROR

# Poems from Japan

Forests and fields, rocks and weeds—my true
companions.
The wild ways of the Crazy Cloud will never
change.
People think I'm mad but I don't care:
If I'm a demon here on earth, there is no need
to fear the hereafter.

—Ikkyu
*Translated by John Stevens*




Who needs the Buddhism of ossified masters?
Me, I've spent three decades alone in the
mountains
And solved all my koans there,
Living Zen among the tall pines and high
winds.

—Ikkyu
*Translated by John Stevens*

# A GENTLEMAN'S WEALTH

A poet's treasure consists of words and phrases;
A scholar's days and nights are perfumed with
      books.
For me, plum blossoms framed by the window
      is an unsurpassable pleasure;
A stomach tight with cold but still enchanted
      by snow, the moon, and dawn frost.

—Ikkyu
*Translated by John Stevens*


For ten straight years, I've reveled in pleasure
      houses.
Now I'm all alone deep in the dark mountain
      valley.
Thirty thousand cloud leagues live between
      me and the places I love.
The only sound that reaches my ears is the
      melancholy wind blowing in the pines.

—Ikkyu
*Translated by John Stevens*

## Basho — From *Back Roads to Far Towns*

Moon and Sun are passing figures of countless genera-
tions, and years coming or going wanderers too. Drifting
life away on a boat or meeting age leading a horse by the
mouth, each day a journey and the journey is home.
Amongst those of old were many that perished upon the
journey. So—when was it—I, drawn like blowing cloud,
couldn't stop dreaming of roaming, roving the coast up
and down, back at the hut last fall by the riverside, sweep-
ing cobwebs off, a year gone and misty skies of spring
returning, yearning to go over the Shirakawa Barrier, pos-
sessed by wanderlust...

Haiku

The summer grass
The mightiest warriors'
Dreams' consequences


So nice and cool
Making myself right at home
Sprawling out for a nap

Silence itself is
In the rock absorbing
Cicada sounds


In the same house
Girls of pleasure also slept
Hagi and moonlight


Merciless indeed
Under the ancient helmet
A cricket crickets


Sweeping the garden
But letting the temple keep
The willows' droppings


*Translated by Cid Corman*

# Haiku of Chiyo-ni

Morning glory—
the well-bucket entangled
I ask for water


Bird's song
left to the world
now it's just the sound of the pine


No more waiting
for the evening or dawn—
touching the old clothes


Clear water is cool
fireflies vanish —
there's nothing more


the autumn wind
resounds in the mountain —
voice of the bell

but for their voices
the herons would disappear —
this morning's snow


one mountain after another
unveiled —
the first mists


at the crescent moon
the silence
enters the heart


sleeping alone
awakened
by the frosty night...

*Translated by Patricia Donegan & Yoshie Ishibashi*

# Haiku of Buson

## SPRING TWILIGHT

Spring is going;
hesitating and indecisive,
the last cherry blossoms.


Reclining Buddha,
its carving just finished,
and the end of spring.


On the hanging bell,
staying while he sleeps,
a butterfly!


A camellia falls,
and the rain of yesterday
spilling out.


Cherry blossoms darkening,
and far way from my home
on a path through fields!

In evening wind—
water is slapping against
legs of a blue heron.


My bones
keep touching against the quilts
in the frosty night!

*Translated by Edith Shiffert & Yuki Sawa*

Evening meditation, enfolded in mountains,
all thought of the world of men dissolve,
Quietly sitting on my cattail cushion
alone, I face the empty window.
Incense burns away, as the dark night deepens,
and my robe is a single fold, as white dew thickens.
Rising from deep meditation, I stroll in the garden,
and the moon is already above the highest peak.

—Ryokan
*Translated by Dennis Maloney & Hide Oshiro*


The water of the mind, how clear it is!
Gazing at it, the boundaries are invisible.
But as soon as even a slight thought arises,
ten thousand images crowd it.
Attach to them and they become real,
be carried by them and it will be difficult to return.
How painful to see a person trapped in the ten-fold delu-
sions.

—Ryokan
*Translated by Dennis Maloney & Hide Oshiro*

What shall remain
as my legacy?
The spring flowers,
the cuckoo in summer,
the autumn leaves.

—Ryokan
*Translated by Dennis Maloney & Hide Oshiro*

## Haiku of Issa

A spring day:
wherever there is water
dusk lingers


A bright full moon
my beatup shack
is as you see it


Eating a meal
alone:
the autumn wind


insects on a branch
floating downstream
still singing


In the cherry blossom's shade
complete strangers
do not exist

Thatched with
morning glory flowers
—my hut

*Translated by Dennis Maloney*

## MOUNTAIN RETREAT

Living deep in the mountains
I've grown fond of the
solitary sound of the singing pines;
On days the wind does not blow,
How lonely it is!

—Rengetsu
*Translated by John Stevens*


## EVENING PLUM BLOSSOMS

As the night advances
the fragrance of the blossoms
Perfumes both the
Sleeves of my black robe
And the recesses of my heart.

—Rengetsu
*Translated by John Stevens*

## MOUNTAIN FALLING FLOWERS

We accept the graceful falling
Of mountain cherry blossoms,
But it is much harder for us
To fall away from our own
Attachment to the world.

—Rengetsu
*Translated by John Stevens*


## STORM DEEP IN THE MOUNTAINS

The roar awakens me from
A peaceful slumber
But then the fierce
Mountain wind blows away
All the dust in my heart.

—Rengetsu
*Translated by John Stevens*

## Haiku of Santoka

No path but this one—
I walk alone.


My begging bowl
accepts the falling leaves.


I have no home;
autumn deepens.


Nothing left to eat;
today's sunrise.


All day I said nothing—
the sound of waves.


Hidden away in
a broken-down hut,
my broken-down life.

*Translated by John Stevens*

If you have time to chatter
Read books
If you have time to read
Walk into mountain, desert and ocean
If you have time to walk
sing songs and dance
If you have time to dance
Sit quietly, you Happy Lucky Idiot

1966 Kyoto

—Nanao Sakaki

# BREAK THE MIRROR

In the morning
After taking cold shower
—what a mistake—
I look in the mirror.

There a funny guy,
Grey hair, white beard, wrinkled skin,
—what a pity—
poor, dirty, old man!
He is not me absolutely not.

Land and life
Fishing in the ocean
Sleeping in the desert with stars
Building a shelter in the mountains
Farming the ancient way
Singing with coyotes
Singing against nuclear war—
I'll never be tired of this life.
Now I'm seventeen years old,
Very charming young man.
I sit down quietly in lotus position,
Meditating, meditating for nothing.
Suddenly a voice comes to me:

"To stay young
to save the world
break the mirror."

October 1981
Canberra, Australia

—Nanao Sakaki

# Along the Silk Road

# Poems from India
# and the Middle East

Lone buck
in the clearing
nearby doe
eyes him with such
longing
that there
in the trees the hunter
seeing his own girl
lets the bow drop

—Anonymous
*Translated by Andrew Schelling*

No one visible up ahead,
no one approaches
from behind.
Not a footprint on the road.
Am I alone?
This much is clear—
the path the ancient
poets opened
is chilled with brush,
and I've long since left
the public thoroughfare.

—Dharmakirti
*Translated by Andrew Schelling*

## VERSE 181

The heart is like a grain of corn, the body like a mill.
But does the mill know why it is turning?

The body is a millstone; its thoughts, the water that turns
the mill.
The millstone says, "The water knows why it is moving."

And the water says, "Ask the miller why.
He's the one who regulates my flow."

And the miller tells you, "Bread-eater, if the mill doesn't
turn
How will there be bread or crumbs for your broth?"

Many things are happening everywhere at once.
Be silent, ask God: He will tell you why.

—Rumi
*Translated by Morton Marcus*

## VERSE 1116

Lovers, O lovers, it is time to break camp and leave the
world.
In my inner ear, the drum of departure is beating from
heaven.

Look, the driver has risen, readied the line of camels
And begged our forgiveness—so why, travelers, are you
still asleep?

All around us are the tinkling of camel bells, the sounds
of departure,
For each moment a soul begins its journey into the void.

From those inverted candles, from those blue awnings
above us,
Wondrous people have come so the mysteries of the
universe may be revealed.

A heavy sleep presses upon you from the circling spheres:
In a life as light as ours, beware of this heavy sleep.

O soul, seek the Beloved; O friend, seek the Friend.
O watchman, be awake, for it is not right that a watchman
should sleep.

Shouting and cursing are everywhere, torches and candles
      in every street,
For tonight this world dies, but from its spasms an eternal
      world is born.


You who were dust are now spirit, you who were ignorant
      are now wise:
The one who led you this far will lead you farther.


The pains he causes you to suffer as he gently draws you
      to him are pleasant.
His flames are like cool water: do not frown at his ways.



His task is to inhabit the soul, his task is to break the vows
      of penitence.
His multiple talents make the atoms tremble at the core.


O ridiculous puppet, you jumped up as if to say, " I am
      King of the Earth."
How long can you jump? Humble yourself or he will bend
      you like a bow.


You planted the seed of deceit, you sneered,
You refused to believe in him: look at you now, O heretic!


Donkey in barn straw, pot with a blackened bottom,

Your place is at the bottom of a well, you disgrace your
      family name.

Someone resides in me who makes my eyes sparkle:
Understand that water scalds because fire heats it.

I have no stone in my hand, I have no quarrel with anyone.
I am harsh with no one, I am sweet as a rose garden.

My eye sees from a different source than yours, from
      another universe.
Here is a world and there is a world: I sit in the threshold
      between them.

The eloquence of those who inhabit this threshold is
      silence.
I have said enough. Rumi, swallow your tongue.

—Rumi
*Translated by Morton Marcus*

# BANKRUPT

If you want me safe, upright and responsible, you're out of
        luck—
I've been drunk on the purest wine from the Day of Alast.

The moment I was first washed clean in Love's cold
        fountain
I pronounced four blessings, on all, for everyone.

Give me wine, and I will tell you more than your fortune.
Her face has made me a lover and her fragrance made me
        drunk.

O reveler, beyond, where the span of a mountain's the
        width of an ant,
do not stop knocking on the door of grace.

He is seen in the rapt gaze of your own reflection—or not
        at all.
Otherwise, under the pale blue dome, no one can be
        happy.

Let my soul be the ransom of your mouth, for in the
        ground of my gaze
the Gardener has planted no rose-bud so beautiful.

Hafiz, from the fortune of your love, has become like
    Solomon,
a bankrupt millionaire, with nothing in his hands but
    wind.

—Hafiz
*Translated by John Slater & Jeffery Einboden*

I have seen an educated man starve,
a leaf blown off by bitter wind.
Once I saw a thoughtless fool
beat his cook.
Lalla has been waiting
for the allure of the world
to fall away.

—Lal Ded
*Translated by Andrew Schelling*

I might scatter the southern clouds,
drain the sea, or cure someone
hopelessly ill.
But to change the mind
of a fool
is beyond me.

—Lal Ded
*Translated by Andrew Schelling*

The god is stone.
The temple is stone.
Top to bottom everything's stone.
What are you praying to,
learned man
Can you harmonize
your five bodily breaths
with the mind?

—Lal Ded
*Translated by Andrew Schelling*

You are the earth, the sky,
the air, the day, the night.
You are the grain
the sandalwood paste
the water, flowers, and all else.
What could I possibly bring
as an offering?

—Lal Ded
*Translated by Andrew Schelling*

I try to imagine my lama's face;
It ought to appear, but doesn't.
I try not to imagine my lover's face;
But clear and bright she shines in my mind.

—The Sixth Dalai Lama
*Translated by Geoffrey Waters*


If a mind obsessed as I am with you
Turned to holy religion,
In one lifetime, in this very body,
Buddhahood indeed!

—The Sixth Dalai Lama
*Translated by Geoffrey Waters*

## GHAZAL 127

Now let me live somewhere with no one,
no one who understands me or my speech.

I'd like to build a doorless, wall-less house,
with nobody for my neighbor, no one for a protector.

Then when I fall sick, no one will be my healer.
When I die, my laments will be sung by no one.

—Ghalib
*Translated by Tony Barnstone*
*and Bilal Shaw*

# GHAZAL 27

My pain comes with no debt to medicine,
but I come out well even if I don't get well.

Why do you gather all my rivals?
I don't complain at the coming spectacle.

Where can I go to test my luck
if you won't come test your dagger on me?

How much sugar is in your lips?
Even when you chide, my rival comes away with no bad
        taste.

Hot news: my lover approaches.
Of all days, I can't come upon a rag in my home!

Nimrod was godlike but what good is that?
My devotion to you comes with no reward.

I give back my life that was given to me,
but fail to come through on my debts.

The wound heals, but the blood isn't stanched.
Once I stop coming to work, work doesn't flow again.

Are you mugging me, or is this a heart-tease?
Come on! Heart-teaser, you flee, taking my heart.

Read something! The people are chattering
Because Ghalib hasn't come to recite his ghazals.

—Ghalib
*Translated by Tony Barnstone*
*and Bilal Shaw*

# I Am Not Empty, I Am Open

## Poems from Europe

# THE WOUNDED MAN

for the wall of a hospital in the front lines

I

The wounded stretch out across the battlefields.
and from that stretched field of bodies that fight
a wheat-field of warm fountains springs up and spreads
out
into streams with husky voices.

Blood always rains upwards towards the sky.
And the wounds lie there making sounds like seashells,
if inside the wounds there is the swiftness of flight,
essence of waves.

Blood smells like the sea, and tastes like the sea, and the
        wine-cellar.
The wine-cellar of the sea, of rough wine, breaks open
where the wounded man drowns, shuddering,
and he flowers and finds himself where he is.

I am wounded: look at me: I need more lives.
The one I have is too small for the consignment
of blood that I want to lose through wounds.
Tell me who has not been wounded.

My life is a wound with a happy childhood.
Pity the man who is not wounded, who doesn't feel
wounded by life, and never sleeps in life,
joyfully wounded.

If a man goes toward the hospitals joyfully,
they change into gardens of half-opened wounds,
of flowering oleanders in front of the surgery room
with its bloodstained doors.


II

Thinking of freedom I bleed, I struggle, manage to live on.
Thinking of freedom, like a tree of blood
that is generous and imprisoned, I give my eyes and hands
to the surgeons.

Thinking of freedom I feel more hearts than grains of
sand
in my chest: my veins give up foam.
and I enter the hospitals and I enter the rolls of gauze
as it they were lilies.

Thinking of freedom I break loose in battle
from those who have rolled her statue through the mud.

And I break loose from my feet, from my arms.
from my house, from everything.

Because where some empty eye-pits dawn,
she will place two stones that see into the future,
and cause new arms and new legs to grow
in the lopped flesh.

Bits of my body I lose in every wound
will sprout once more, sap-filled, autumnless wings.
Because I am like the lopped tree, and I sprout again:
because I still have my life.


—Miguel Hernandez
*Translated by James Wright*

# THE MOST FRAGILE THING IS WHAT ENDURES

Your youth? It's no more
Than a scent of orange blossoms

In a little plaza some evening
When the light is fading

And a streetlamp is coming on.
You smell its perfume

Thrown up from a past
That was yours yesterday, remote today,

Enveloping you: a fragrance
Singular and immemorial

Of everything, your blood,
The loves and friendships

Of your first existence,
When whatever you desired

Would soon be made real
By time in that new

Future; a fragrance
Furtive as a shadow,

Stirring your senses
With a chill.

And you see the deepest thing
In your life is no more than a wisp

Of what so many sensible people
Would call nothing:

A scent of orange blossoms, air.
Was there ever anything more?

—Luis Cernuda
*Translated by Stephen Kessler*

## PORTRAIT

My childhood is memories of a patio in Seville,
and a sunny orchard where lemons ripen;
my youth, twenty years on the soil of Castile;
my story, a few events just as well forgotten.

I was never a great seducer or Don Juan
—that is apparent by my shabby dress—
but I was struck by the arrow Cupid aimed at me
and loved whenever I was welcomed.

Despite the Jacobin blood in my veins,
my poems bubble up from a calm spring;
and more than a man who lives by rules
I am, in the best sense of the word, good.

I adore beauty and following modern aesthetics,
I've cut old roses from Ronsard's garden;
but I hate being fashionable
and am no bird strutting the latest style.

I shun the shallow tenors' ballads
and the chorus of crickets singing at the moon;
I stop to separate the voices from the echoes,
and I listen among the voices to only one.

Am I classical or romantic? I don't know. I want
to leave my poetry as the captain leaves his sword:
remembered for the virile hand that gripped it,
not for the hallmark of its maker.

I converse with the man who is always with me,
—he who talks to himself hopes to talk to God some-
day—
my soliloquy is a discussion with this friend,
who taught me the secret of loving others.

In the end I owe you nothing; you owe me all I've written.
I work, paying with what I've earned
for the clothes on my back, the house I inhabit,
the bread that sustains me, and the bed where I lie.

And when the day arrives for the final voyage
and the ship of no return is set to sail,
you'll find me aboard, traveling light, with few possessions,
almost naked, like the children of the sea.

—Antonio Machado
*Translated by Mary Berg & Dennis Maloney*

# FROM *PROVERBS*

Traveler, your footprints
are the only road, nothing else.
Traveler, there is no road;
you make your own path as you walk.
As you walk, you make your own road,
and when you look back
you see the path
you will never travel again.
Traveler, there is no road;
only a ship's wake on the sea.


It is good to know that glasses
are to drink from;
the bad thing is that we don't know
what thirst is for.


Man has four things
that are no good at sea;
anchor, rudder, oars,
and the fear of going down.

—Antonio Machado
*Translated by Mary Berg & Dennis Maloney*

SEAS

  I feel my boat
has struck something large
there, in the depths of the sea!

        And then nothing
happens! Nothing...Silence... Waves...

  Nothing happens? Or has everything happened
And are we now, calm, in someplace new?

—Juan Ramon Jimenez
*Translated by Mary Berg & Dennis Maloney*

## ROUTE

Below, everyone is asleep,
                              Above, alert,
the ship's pilot and I.

            He watches the compass, in charge
of our bodies, under lock
and key. I, with my eyes
on the infinite, steering
the open treasures of our souls.

—Juan Ramon Jimenez
*Translated by Mary Berg & Dennis Maloney*

# VERMEER

No protected world...Just behind the wall the noise
        begins,
the inn is there
with laughter and bickering, rows of teeth, tears, the din of
        bells
and the deranged brother-in-law, the death-bringer we all
        must tremble for.

The big explosion and the tramp of rescue arriving late
the boats preening themselves on the straits, the money
        creeping down
in the wrong man's pocket
demands stacked on demands
gaping red flowerheads sweating premonitions of war.

In from there and right through the wall into the clear
        studio
into the second that's allowed to live for centuries.
Pictures that call themselves "The Music Lesson"
or "Woman in Blue Reading a Letter"—
she's in her eighth month, two hearts kicking inside her.
On the wall behind is a crumpled map of Terra Incognita.

Breathe calmly...An unknown blue material nailed to the
        chairs.

The gold studs flew in with incredible speed
and stopped abruptly
as if they had never been other than stillness.

Ears sing, from depth or height.
It's the pressure from the other side of the wall.
It makes each fact float
and steadies the brush.

It hurts to go through walls, it makes you ill
but it is necessary.
The world is one. But walls...
And the wall is part of yourself—
we know or we don't know but it's true for us all
except for small children. No walls for them.

The clear sky has leant itself against the wall.
It's like a prayer to the emptiness.
And the emptiness turns its face to us
and whispers
'I am not empty, I am open.'

—Tomas Transtromer
*Translated by Robin Fulton*

# ROMANESQUE ARCHES

Inside the huge romanesque church the tourists jostled in
       the half darkness.
Vault gaped behind vault, no complete view.
A few candle-flames flickered.
An angel with no face embraced me
and whispered through my whole body:
"Don't be ashamed of being human, be proud!
Inside you vault opens behind vault endlessly.
You will never be complete, that's how it's meant to be."
Blind with tears
I was pushed out on the sun-seething piazza
together with Mr. and Mrs. Jones, Mr. Tanaka and Signora
       Sabatini
and inside them all vault opened behind vault endlessly.

—Tomas Transtromer
*Translated by Robin Fulton*

## WHEN WE SLEEP

We are all children when we sleep.
There's no war in us then.
We open our hands and breathe
in that calm rhythm heaven has given us.

We all let go of our lips like small children
and open our hands halfway,
soldiers and statesmen, servants and masters.
The stars stand guard and
form a haze across the vaults
—a few hours when none shall do each other harm.

If we could only speak to each other then
when our hearts are like half-open flowers.
Words like golden bees
would slip through.
—God, teach me the language of sleep.

—Rolf Jacobsen
*Translated by Olav Grinde*

## ASPHALT

First they come with grey gravel
and then they come with black asphalt.
First it's like silk.
Then like steel.

Because everything has to be strong and hard now,
and level of course,
and naked and perfectly smooth
so they can come rolling forth, first on silent rubber.
Then on belts of iron.

First you must learn to keep quiet.
Then you must have the correct opinions.
First it concerns your thoughts.
Then your hopes and dreams.

—Rolf Jacobsen
*Translated by Olav Grinde*

## PROBLEM II

...whatever we do
the machines
only move the hunger two stairs up;
now it sits in the heart.

—Rolf Jacobsen
*Translated by Olav Grinde*

# BREATHING EXERCISE

If you go far enough out
you can only see the sun as a spark
in a dying fire
if you go far enough out.

If you go far enough out
you can see the entire wheel of the Milky Way
roll away on roads of night
if you go far enough out.

If you go far enough out
you can see the Universe itself,
all the billion light years summed up time
only as a flash, just as lonely, as distant


as a star on a June night
if you go far enough out.

and still, my friend, if you go far enough out
you are only at the beginning

—of yourself.

—Rolf Jacobsen
*Translated by Olav Grinde*

# TRUTH

Truth waits outside your door.
Dressed in rags, She is ill.
She has a child on her arm. She wants in.
Do you hear the dogs barking? She is afraid.
What do you do? If you open
it will change your life.

Do you hesitate?
You, too.

—Rolf Jacobsen
*Translated by Olav Grinde*

# T'AO CH'IEN

If one day T'ao Ch'ien
came to visit me, I
would show him my cherry and apple trees,
and I'd prefer him to come in spring
when they're in blossom. Then we'll sit in the shade
with a glass of cider, perhaps, I'll show him
a poem—if I can find one he'd like.
The dragons that blaze across the sky trailing poison and
smoke
soared more quietly in his time, and more birds sang.
There's nothing here he'd not understand.
More than ever he'd want to retire
to a little garden like this.
But I don't know if he'd do so with a good conscience.

—Olav Hauge
*Translated By Robin Fulton*

EVERYDAY

You've left the big storms
behind you now.
You didn't ask then
why you were born,
where you came from, where you were going to,
you were just there in the storm,
in the fire.
But it's possible to live
in the everyday as well,
in the grey quiet day,
set potatoes, rake leaves,
carry brushwood.
There's so much to think about here in the world,
one life is not enough for it all.
After work you can fry pork
and read Chinese poems.
Old Laertes cut briars,
dug round his fig trees,
and let the heroes fight on at Troy.

—Olav Hauge
*Translated by Robin Fulton*

After all, why sadness? Why fear? We don't know the depths of Finnish lakes, the cold of the Siberian taiga, the map of the Gobi desert. We don't even know what's in your dreams. Mine, too. That's the way it is. But you, as always; listening in the dark, lighting matches, gazing straight ahead. The man whose name you won't forget—even in the middle of the night—still hasn't called. You're hungry. In the corner of the room an old man in a rocking chair creaks back and forth, the shining keys of the sax laid on its side reflect your soft face, which you hide from yourself and others. Framed by the window, horses hover above the ground, wandering aimlessly through men's destinies, silk tails sailing in the wind. And for a moment, while the old man leans over a book—leafed through hundreds of times—you see the riders galloping across the fields, through the woods, heads down, black hair waving in the setting sun, the vanishing sun. Gone. Is that why you can't remember the short poem describing the whole world as it was and will be, why dusk blinds you to the stories of everyone, stories known only to the man whose name you won't forget—even in the middle of the night, the man who stands somewhere in the open, alone, in the dark, on the high plains?

—Ales Debeljak
*Translated by Christopher Merrill & the Author*

Your story's simple. You won't see many loved ones when you return, like an otter surfacing in a lake to catch its breath. You won't find words for short greetings, the seasons, unsuccessful missions, white phosphorus lighting the passion in soldiers' eyes, a distant whistle on steep hillsides you never climbed, children's cane baskets floating silently across a river basin, the way you have a constant burning pain, the constellations discovered in a premonition, Oriental love songs, the disappointment of everything we were and will be. Believe me: this is your story. Later, I'll tell it again—only better.

—Ales Debeljak
*Translated by Christopher Merrill & the Author*

# BE DRUNK

Be drunk always! That is the only question; That's it! Be drunk without truce.
Not to feel the painful burden of Time, which bruises your shoulders and bends you down to the ground.

Drunk with what? With wine, with poetry or with virtue, as you like, but be drunk!

And if sometimes, on the steps of a palace, in the green grass of a ditch, or in the gloomy solitude of your room, you should wake up with your drunkenness half-gone or vanished,
ask the wind and the waves, the star, the bird, the clock, ask all that flies, all that groans,
all that flows, all that sings, all that speaks.

Ask them what time it is: and the wind, the wave, the star, the bird, and the clock will answer, "It's time to be drunk! If you are not to be the tormented slave of Time, get drunk, be drunk always! With wine, with poetry, or with virtue, as you like."

—Charles Baudelaire
*Translated by Hide and Catherine Oshiro*

# TO SILENCE

It is so still now, full of night.
The cat's asleep and his tail is quiet.
The minutes burn like hissing matches.
Four-footed moments brush by
through consciousness. They stare at me
while I, an early riser, season a gray workday
with a smoke.

Small sounds make the silence clearer,
make it something other than a surface.
Here I sit and listen to nothing.
It is good to hear the silence,
the great depth where all exists,
where all that exists becomes something.

A pencil is rasping out words.
The cat's paws quiver in sleep.
He dreams of ten birds in a tree.
I dream of a passion with twenty wings.
Lead is dull. Blood is quick.
A red silence runs in my body.

—Tommy Olofsson
*Translated by Jean Pearson*

# YOUR WORDS

Your words
I will read
like the blind read:
with my fingertips
search my way
word for word, toward you.

With my eyes, I see
only the written sign.
My senses and skin,
perhaps my memory of you
let me feel you near,
recognize you,
know you

when I drink in your words
through thirsty, thirsty
fingertips—

—Halldis Moren Vesass
*Translated by Ron Wakefield*

## ARCHAIC TORSO OF APOLLO

We cannot know his mythic head, the eyes
like apples ripening among the leaves.
But his torso's glowing lamp achieves
an effect, though turned low, to mesmerize—

the way his glance glimmers within—else still
the bow of the breast could not dazzle you,
nor, in turning, could a smile play through
those loins, centering procreation's will.

Else this stone would seem stunted and defiled
and could not shimmer so, like a wild
beast's fur beneath the shoulder's lucid fall,

and it would not burst from itself so rife
with flame, star-like, for there is no place at all
that does not see you. You must change your life.

—Rainer Maria Rilke
*Translated by Joe Cadora*

# THE PANTHER

From endless passing of the bars his gaze
Has grown so weary that it now resists
All else. There seem a thousand bars, a haze,
And beyond those thousand bars no world exists.

The soft pad of his strong, sinuous pace
Turns in constricted circles there until,
Like a mighty dance around the smallest space,
It centers a numb but still enormous will.

Only sometimes the shades of the pupils rise,
Silently, and an image enters where they part;
Through his tense, unmoving limbs it flies
Till it ceases to exist within his heart.

—Rainier Maria Rilke
*Translated by Joe Cadora*

# LACQUER

Destiny rolls over me. Sometimes like an egg. Sometimes
With its paws, slamming me into the slope. I shout. I take
My stand. I pledge all my juices. I shouldn't
Do this. Destiny can snuff me out, I feel it now.

If destiny doesn't blow on our souls, we freeze
Instantly. I spend days and days afraid
The sun wouldn't rise. That this was my last day.
I felt light sliding from my hands, and if I didn't

Have enough quarters in my pocket, and Metka's voice
Were not sweet enough and kind and solid and
Real, my soul would escape from my body, one day

It will. With death you have to be kind.
Home is where we're from. Everything in a moist
dumpling.
We live only for a flash. Until the lacquer dries.

—Tomaz Salamun
*Translated by Christopher Merrill*

# Between Stone
## and Ocean

# Poems from Latin America

# HOUSE

Perhaps this is the house I lived in
when neither I nor earth existed,
when all was moon or stone or darkness,
when still light was unborn.
Perhaps then this stone was
my house, my windows or my eyes.
This rose of granite reminds me
of something that dwelled in me or I in it,
a cave, or cosmic head of dreams,
cup or castle, ship or birth.
I touch the stubborn spirit of rock,
its rampart pounds in the brine,
and my flaws remain here,
wrinkled essence that rose
from the depths to my soul,
and stone I was, stone I will be. Because of this
I touch this stone, and for me it hasn't died:
it's what I was, what I will be, resting
from a struggle long as time.

—Pablo Neruda
*Translated by Dennis Maloney*

# I WILL RETURN

Some other time, man or woman, traveler,
later, when I am not alive,
look here, look for me
between stone and ocean,
in the light storming
through the foam.
Look here, look for me,
for here I will return, without saying a thing,
without voice, without mouth, pure,
here I will return to be the churning
of the water, of
its unbroken heart,
here, I will be discovered and lost:
here, I will, perhaps, be stone and silence.

—Pablo Neruda
*Translated by Dennis Maloney*

# THE BODY

What would the body of Saint Francis be like? They say it was so delicate that it might have disappeared in the wind. It cast very little shadow: one's shadow is like pride in earthly possessions, like the shadow of a tree painting the grass, or the shadow of a woman who passes through a fountain and is instantly drenched. The humble one hardly cast a shadow.

He was small in stature. Just like a whitecap crossing the water, he traveled and sensed the presence that watched over his body.

His arms were light, so light. He did not feel them at his sides when they dropped. His head was like the small stamen inside a flower.

He walked gracefully: his legs passed lightly over the grass without trampling it, and his chest was narrow, although wide for love (love is the essence and not water which requires great vessels!) And his shoulders...they were narrowed by humility; they made one think of a very small cross, one smaller than the other.

His sides were burned to a slenderness. The flesh of youth had vanished, along with its sins.

Perhaps his small body crackled, just as dry cactuses crackle with heat.

Human happiness is something like pregnancy; he did not want it. Pain is another thicket of conquests, and he fled from it. His heavenly pleasure and sustenance was the love of animals. He tended to see the world as a place as light as a flower. And he, resting within his own boundaries, did not want to weigh more than a nectar-seeking bee.

Who sings better in the valleys when the wind passes? Those with fat ears say it is the river that shatters goblets in the gravel; others say it is a woman who refines a cry in her fleshy throat.

But the best cry comes from the small, empty vehicle, where there are no inner organs for the voice to be hindered, and this small car, guided through the valleys, is you, little Francis, the one who has hardly made his mark on the world. You are like a small, slim shadow.

—Gabriela Mistral
*Translated by Maria Jacketti*

## THE FIG

Touch me: it is the softness of good satin, and when you open me, what an unexpected rose! Do you not remember some king's black cloak under which a redness burned?

I bloom inside myself to enjoy myself with an inward gaze, scarcely for a week.

Afterward, the satin generously opens in a great fold of long Congolese laughter.

Poets have not known the color of night, nor the Palestinian fig. We are both the most ancient blue, a passionate blue, which richly concentrates itself because of its ardor.

If I spill my pressed flowers into your hand, I create a dwarf meadow for your pleasure; I shower you with the meadow's bouquet until covering your feet. No. I keep the flowers tied—they make me itch; the resting rose also knows this sensation.

I am also the pulp of the rose-of-Sharon, bruised.

Allow my praise to be made: the Greeks were nourished by me, and they have praised me less than Juno, who gave them nothing.

—Gabriela Mistral
*Translated by Maria Jacketti*

# THE MOST UNBELIEVABLE PART

The most unbelievable part,
they were people like us
good manners
well-educated and refined.
Versed in abstract sciences,
always took a box for the Symphony
made regular trips to the dentist
attended very nice prep schools
some played golf...

Yes, people like you, like me
family men
grandfathers
uncles and godfathers.

But they went crazy
delighted in burning
children and books
played at decorating cemeteries
bought furniture  made of broken bones
dined on tender ears and testicles.

Though they were invincible
meticulous in their duties
and spoke of torture

in the language of surgeons and butchers.

They assassinated the young of my country
and of yours.
now nobody could believe in Alice through the looking
glass
now nobody could stroll along the avenues
without terror bursting through their bones.

And the most unbelievable part
they were people
like you
like me
yes, nice people
just like us.

—Marjorie Agosin
*Translated by Cola Franzen*

# HOW DOES AN IMPRISONED WOMAN
SEE THE LIGHT?

The imprisoned woman on the threshold
dreams of the light
senses it surrounding her
along with names and
clearings that
go beyond colors.
She plays, with the light
insatiable, morning-like and many colored
while rousing
those who love one another
calling up a memory
of bonfires.

She asks for a sliver of light
demands light so as
not to forget hands extended
open free of sleeplessness and crimes
light to become languid, to mingle with her hair
the texture of her fissured arms.

The prisoner on the threshold
dreams of the light
and sombered among blindfolds
obscured in complicitious cells

she summons up the light
invents a sliver of gold
in the midst of laments.

—Marjorie Agosin
*Translated by Cola Franzen*

# THE HAND'S GESTURE

The hand's gesture
when it tries to write
sometimes creates thought,
creates the image
that then moves the hand.

A gesture also creates love,
which then creates other gestures
and something else that's underneath.

The independent language of gestures
appears a calculated chance
to awaken the latent waiting
that lives in the depth of everything.

Also the tree is a language of gestures
where chance and the tree's complicity
unite so that a leaf may fall.

—Roberto Juarroz
*Translated by Mary Crow*

# THE MOST BEAUTIFUL DAY

The most beautiful day
lacks something:
its dark side.
Only to a near-sighted god
could light by itself
appear beautiful.

Beside any Let there light!,
Let there be shadow!
Should also be said.

We don't arrive
at necessary night by omission.

—Roberto Juarroz
*Translated by Mary Crow*

# BREATHING LESSONS

## Poems from
## the United States

# THE SUPPLE DEER

The quiet opening
between fence strands
perhaps eighteen inches.

Antlers to hind hooves,
four feet off the ground,
the deer poured through.

No tuft of the coarse white belly hair left behind.

I don't know how a stag turns
into a stream, an arc of water.
I have never felt such accurate envy.

Not of the deer:

To be that porous, to have such largeness pass through me.

—Jane Hirshfield

# FIRMAMENT

Fish in the sky of water—silverly
as traveling moon through cloud-hills—
down current whisks, or deeper
fins into depths, to rise or sagely
wait in the milky mist of
disturbed sediment, wheeling briskly
at least whim, at one
with the aqueous everything it shines in.

—Denise Levertov

# YOU ASK ME ABOUT BIRDS AND I TELL YOU

if sometimes, when a heron
spread her great wings to dry
in whatever sun there was I
thought of you, the hidden strength
unfolding from your body,

and if, watching hawks work
through air so still only the sunlit tips
of their wings moved, like fingers,
I remembered the tips of your fingers
in their slow love circles, oh

yes, and if I've noticed
how a raven's wings luff
overhead like spilled breath,
how an owl's scoop air without sound
in its quickest flight,

it was to understand this,
our coming together, the way
pine siskins leave a tree, suddenly, all
at once, and between their startled wings
those drunken patches of light.

—Samuel Green

## VIOLENCE ON TELEVISION

It is best to turn on the set only after all the stations have gone off the air and just watch the snowfall. This is the other life you have been promising yourself; somewhere back in the woods, ten miles from the nearest town, and that just a wide place in the road with a tavern and a gas station. When you drive home, after midnight, half drunk, the roads are treacherous. And your wife is home alone, worried, looking anxiously out at the snow. This snow has been falling steadily for days, so steadily the snow plows can't keep up. So you drive slow, peering down the road. And there! Did you see it? Just as the edge of your head-light beams, something, a large animal, or a man, crossed the road. Stop. There he is among the birches, a tall man wearing a white suit. No, it isn't a man. Whatever it is it motions to you, almost human gesture, than retreats far-ther into the woods. He stops and motions again. The snow is piling up all around the car. Are you coming?

—Louis Jenkins

# LIFE IS SO COMPLEX

Life is so complex even though you eat brown rice and brush your teeth with baking soda. Simplify, spend the day alone. Spend it fishing. Watch the line and the motion of the water, your thoughts drift...then there is a slight bump and a steady pull on the line and the whole line of cars begins to move as the train pulls out of the station. Someone takes the seat beside you, someone at the end of a love affair. The threats of murder and suicide, the pleading, the practical jokes, became at the end only tiresome and she is relieved at his going. She turns away before the train is out of sight.

Your ordinary life is simple, full of promise, bullet-like, pushing aside the waves of air, moving with incredible speed toward the life that waits, motionless, unsuspecting, at the heart of the forest.

—Louis Jenkins

# EPIPHANY

It happens not so much on schedule
as at those moments when
something with something else
beautifully collides.

Nelson taking the ball from Mitchell
on a fast break, for example,
then stopping suddenly short
to break the school record from twenty feet,
the ball at the height of its high soft arc
like a full moon fully risen.

Or the student in Composition
reading aloud the surprising words
of her essay,
weeping at the new loss
of something lost a long time ago,
the eyes of the boy on the back row
saying I must have been blind—
she's wonderful.

The ball descending then
to flounce the net
like a rayon skirt,

the young man on the back row
studying his hands
as if learning
for the first time ever
what they might be holding.

—William Kloefkorn

## BUGS IN A BOWL

Han Shan, that great and crazy, wonder-filled
Chinese poet of a thousand years ago, said:

We're just like bugs in a bowl. All day
going around never leaving their bowl.

I say, That's right! Every day climbing up
the steep sides, sliding back.

Over and over again. Around and around.
up and back down.

Sit in the bottom of the bowl, head in your hands,
cry, moan, feel sorry for yourself.

Or. Look around. See your fellow bugs,
Walk around.

Say, Hey, how you doin'?
Say, Nice bowl!

—David Budbill

# BEN

You can see him in the village almost anytime.
He's always on the street.
At noon he ambles down to Jerry's
in case a trucker who's stopped by for lunch
might feel like buying him a sandwich.
Don't misunderstand, Ben's not starving;
he's there each noon because he's sociable
not because he's hungry.
He is a friend to everyone except the haughty.

There are at least half a dozen families in the village
who make sure he always has enough to eat
and there are places
where he's welcome to come in and spend the night.

Ben is a cynic in the Greek and philosophic sense,
one who gives his life to simplicity
seeking only the necessities
so he can spend his days
in the presence of his dreams.

Ben is a vision of another way,
the vessel in this place
for bhikkhu, thera, Taoist hermit,
Ancient Christian mystic of the Egyptian desert

Chuang Tzu, The Abbot Moses, Meister Eckhart,
Chatral, Khamtul Rimpoche, Thomas Merton—
all these and all the others live in Ben, because
in America only a dog
can spend his days
on the street or by the river
in quiet contemplation
and be fed.

—David Budbill

# HYMNUS AD PATREM SINENSIS

I praise those ancient Chinamen
who left me a few words,
usually a pointless joke or a silly question
A line of poetry drunkenly scrawled on the margin
of a quick splashed picture—bug, leaf,
caricature of Teacher—
On paper held together now by little more than ink
their own strength brushed momentarily over it

Their world and several others since
Gone to hell in a handbasket, they knew it—
Cheered as it whizzed by—
conked out among the busted spring rain cherry blossom
winejars
Happy to have saved us all.

31:VIII:58

—Philip Whalen

# A LETTER TO PHILIP (WHALEN)

can i any longer address you dear phil
when i have spent the morning
ordering my life in unrealities

the rent the food the clothing
the ten percent allowed for luxuries
the baseball register and the sporting news

which things are necessary in my world i say

i have written my oldest son
and sent a check to celebrate his nineteenth year
and i have yelled at  my youngest son
to celebrate his curiosity which stalled my writing checks

my head is awhirl with money and games and family
and you are in the real world finally

now you are not only my brother
but the world's brother and the ant's brother
god's brother and even the foolish writer's brother

which is why i wonder how i dare start a letter dear phil
wanting to know the honorific when you must recognize
none such

but there is a need to honor you somehow
as you honor me by every step you take

i think of you sitting silent sitting speaking walking
and i am honored
       i have been given this grace to know a decent man
who does right things while i whirl in unrealities
writing checks and poems

—Joel Oppenheimer

## MAPLE BRIDGE NIGHT-MOORING

Moon sets, a crow caws,
        frost fills the sky
River, Maple, fishing-fires
        cross my troubled sleep.
Beyond the walls of Suzhou
        from Cold Mountain temple
The midnight bell sounds
        reach my boat.

Zhang-ji
Translated by Gary Snyder

At Maple Bridge

Men are mixing gravel and cement
At Maple bridge,
Down an alley by a tea-stall
From Cold Mountain temple;
Where Zhang Ji heard the bell.
The stone step moorage
Empty, lapping water,
And the bell sound has traveled
Far across the sea.

—Gary Snyder

I saw myself
a ring of bone
in the clear stream
of all of it

and vowed,
always to be open to it
that all of it
might flow through

and then heard
"ring of bone" where
ring is what a
bell does

—Lew Welch

## DIFFICULTY ALONG THE WAY

Seeking Perfect Total Enlightenment
Is looking for a flashlight
When all you needed the flashlight for
Is to find your flashlight

—Lew Welch

## MISSING A GOOD FRIEND GONE FAR

Perhaps this letter will cross
with one from you, catch fire in heaven, find its way
to your brushwood shack, the boiling roots and seeping
tea.

Maybe you're on your way back, throat singing
with a Mongolian bride. Or gone further in,
rattling the two heads of your drum,
riding auroras of timeless light.

Here, I'm saturated with papers and ink,
empty tracks this way and that. Snow on chokecherries,
broken roof to let in the breeze.

The whole country's on its knees, manipulated
with threats of an invisible enemy. Everything I want to say
is subject to exam, letters opened, words scanned.

My shoes are off, too heavy with mud.
I'll postmark this from a cave, with a willow stick
dipped in cinnabar.

Write me in return, or come see me
after you've gone deeper, your chin full of hair,
your eyes grown out of your head.

—John Brandi

## SHADOW PLAY

Doubt fuels us,
faith keeps the body in place.
No word approximates the fire
that shapes the wind.

Silence surrounds us
like pounding rain.

We rise into a world
of heated verbs, sacrifice
the alphabet on a moving bough
of leaves.

What we write is shadow play,
pollen sifting
from the body's tree.

—John Brandi

# BAMIYAN

in the pink sandstone cliffs
of the Koh-e Baba Mountains,

spent rocket casing,
steel support rods &

shrapnel surround a pair
of yawning outlines

carved from rock, cave
murals coated in dust &

soot, a spray-painted phrase
from the sacred Koran:

the just replaces the unjust

assailed by artillery
& heavy canon fire,

faces hacked off,
then dynamited under

Talib rule &
yet it remains: nothing

can't be blown up

—Shin Yu Pai

# IRIS

I transplanted iris bulbs along the wall of the garage,
almost in the alley. No one can see them there except
the garbage men as they fling cans in and out of their
        truck.
The neighbor says they're so thick it's a wonder they can
        bloom.
Hundreds of deep purple blossoms, the purple vibrating
        against
the green stalks and leaves, the pale blue wall of
        the building.
Even the air around the flowers shimmers and clings.
        The hose
won't reach so I haul water in a bucket, again and again,
standing, watching the water rise then walking carefully,
lopsided, a little water splashing out onto my legs as I go.
The Buddhist monks stand in lines—long lines going
        back
row after row, deep human. They slide forward, barely
lifting their soft feet from the ground. Facing them,
at the end of the muddy street, are the police, in helmets,
with guns, or soldiers, or members of the rubber workers
union, or brothers and sisters of civil servants or students
from the university that has been closed, everyone dressed
in neat black pants and white shirts, and there are the
        monks,

shaved heads bobbing on thin necks. Before the crowd,
      they stop
and sit down in the road. I can smell the sweat from
      beneath
their arms and the perfume that saturates their spotless
      robes.

—David Romtvedt

# WILD STRAWBERRY

And I rode the Greyhound down to Brooklyn
Where I sit now eating woody strawberries
Grown on the backs of Mexican farmers
Imported from the fields of their hands,
Juices without color or sweetness

    My wild blood berries of spring meadows
    Sucked by June bees and protected by hawks
    Have stained my face and honeyed
    My tongue... healed the sorrow of my flesh

    Vines crawl across the grassy floor
    Of the north, scatter to the world
    Seeking the light of the sun and innocent
    Tap of the rain to feed the roots
    And bud small white flowers that in June
    Will burst fruit and announce spring
    When wolf will drop winter fur
    And wrens will break the egg

    My blood, blood berries that brought laughter
    And the ache in the stooped back that vied
    With dandelions for the plucking,
    And the vines nourished our youth and heralded
    Iris, corn, and summer melon

We fought bluebirds for the seeds
Armed against garter snakes, field mice;
Won the battle with the burning sun
Which blinded our eyes and froze out hands
To the vines and the earth where knees knelt
And we laughed in the morning dew like worms
And grubs; we scented age and wisdom

My mother wrapped the wounds of the world
With a sassafras poultice and we ate
Wild berries with their juice running
Down the roots of our mouth and our joy

I sit here in Brooklyn eating Mexican
Berries which I did not pick, nor do
I know the hands which did, nor their stories...
January snowfalls, listen...

—Maurice Kenny

# BLACK MARSH ECLOGUE

Although it is midsummer, the great blue heron
holds darkest winter in his hunched shoulders,
those blue-turning-gray clouds
rising over him like a storm from the Pacific.

He stands in the black marsh
more monument than bird, a wizened prophet
returned from a vanished mythology.
He watches the hearts of things

and does not move or speak. But when
at last he flies, his great wings
cover the darkening sky, and slowly,
as though praying, he lifts, almost motionless,

as he pushes the world away.

—Sam Hamill

# DESCENT

down gently
through the smokehole down
sky to water gourd
     down
into shadows down
     as a child
is being born
     and close
          by fire
an elder is huddled
awaiting the calm journey
     down
and sparks
     are star patterns
of dew upon webs
which descend
     and hang
to drop
     upon
          a drum's taut surface.

—Peter Blue Cloud

FOR HARRY

THE
MILKY
WAY
IS
another
shiny
cricket
chirping
while leaves
fall

—Michael McClure

FOR NORMA

NOTH
ING
NESS
of
intelligence;
silver
sunlight
through
closed
eyelids

—Michael McClure

The stars are there not
to remind us but to let
us know what this is.

There is no end and
            never was a beginning—so
here we are—amidst.


Nothing ends with you—
every leaf on the ground
remembering root.

—Cid Corman

# O LENTE, LENTE, CURRITE NOCTIS EQUI

We take our time
it is not fun
we take it
but we don't have it
we take
each other's
time
do we waste it?
We take our own
sweet time.
We have to.
There is no time to waste.
It seems to go away,
but
it is always here/
always
Now.
it is still here.
it is still
here.
We don't do anything yet.
We do it now.
We wait for it.
We take out time.
We hold our breath.

We take our time.

—Robin Kay Willoughby

PETALS
for Marcia

I spilled the flowers
Pale pink petals

Funny
what can scare
you in this world

one day
pale pink petals
scattered on the table

another day
gray-black petals
three little shadows

spilled, scattered
backlit on
the shiny film
there!
in the lower left lobe

I reach for

your fingertips

pale pink petals
brush
my cheek

This world—

Funny
how
in the light of death
everything
shines!

—Rick Fields

## MULADHARA: 4

We are older than dirt.
All death comes to dirt to die.
Rooting around in the compost
made from kitchen scraps and old letters
I feel its black and writhing warmth.
It is alive with what eats and excretes,
a snake full of snakes, black snake
with its mouth open, mouth from which
can be charmed honeysuckle, peppers, the climbing rose,
or into which I could fall
and myself be digested, transformed
into something blue and fragrant.

This snake's mouth is wide open
but stuffed with its own tail.
What song could I sing
that would call it up?
What song more fascinating
than this song of itself?

—Sherry Robbins

## RELATIVITY

We move on the Earth
As it moved through us,
Keeping pace like the moon does
As we rush along a country road,
Its pale circle streaming beside us
Through the night.

Thus we stretch the minutes
Pointing toward our deaths,
Extend the flicker granted
To the molecules that know
The road we're on.

And when we stop in the shadow
Of a mountain to catch our breath,
The mountain keeps going
Through the atoms of our flesh.

—Penny Harter

## OF DEAFNESS

Each man has a quiet that revolves
around him as he beats his head against the earth. But I am
laughing

hard and furious. I pour a glass of pepper vodka
and toast to the white wall. I say we were

never silent. We read each other's lips to uncover
the poverty of laughter. And whoever listens to me: being

there, and not being, lost and found
and lost again: Thank you for the feather on my tongue,

thank you for our argument that ends,
thank you for my deafness, Lord, such fire

from a match you never lit.

—Ilya Kaminsky

# THE ROSHI'S REPLY

Dreaming? Yes, you are dreaming.
This world is a dream, but not a frivolous one.
Each of us dreams a part of this dream
which was dreamt before our parents were born,
and each of our dreams, opening ahead of us,
hollows out a little more of the universe,
until a network of paths radiates among the stars,
paths like shafts of light, like facets in a diamond.

The entrance to your path is anywhere you turn,
and each step along it as natural as breathing.
Follow this path and soon it will seem
as familiar as the garden walkway behind your home,
for you will have found your path in the original dream
where all paths are contained and revealed as One.

It is like a cut-glass bowl on a moonlit night
when we can no longer tell the sparkling container
from the glittering water it contains.
Do you see? There is nothing to get excited about.
We are talking about an ordinary glass bowl.
Just a bowl. And water, just water. And yet, and yet...

—Morton Marcus

# FINDING THE FATHER

Someone knocks on the door; we do not have time to dress. He wants us to come with him through the blowing and rainy streets, to the dark house. We will go there, the body says, and there find the father whom we have never met, who wandered in a snowstorm the night we were born, who then lost his memory, and has lived since longing for his child, whom he saw only once . . . while he worked as a shoemaker, as a cattle herder in Australia, as a restaurant cook who painted at night. When you light the lamp you will see him. He sits there behind the door . . . the eyebrows so heavy, the forehead so light . . . lonely in his whole body, waiting for you.

—Robert Bly

# LIKE THE NEW MOON I WILL LIVE MY LIFE

When your privacy is beginning over,
how beautiful the things are that you did not notice before!
A few sweetclover plants
along the road to Bellingham,
culvert ends poking out of driveways,
wooden corncribs, slowly falling
what no one loves, no one rushes towards or shouts about,
what lives like the new moon,
and the wind
blowing against the rumps of grazing cows.

Telephone wires stretched across water,
a drowning sailor standing at the foot of his mother's bed
grandfathers and grandsons sitting together.

—Robert Bly

## QUANTUM PEARLS

Now it's the New Physics that tell us we don't die
at death, the body recomposes into something
rich and strange, a quantum exchange of atoms—
incandescent starlight, emerald fire in wave crest—
what Shakespeare knew all along—of his bones
are coral made, those are pearls that were his eyes.

—Joe Stroud

## LOST IN TRANSLATION

The ten thousand leaves of the Man'yoshu.
Page after page of mist, and dew, and tears.
All those poems with their exquisite grief.
And how hard to tell from the translation
which sorrows are merely literary, which
written in an ink crushed from the heart.

—Joe Stroud

# SURPRISED BY MY OWN HANDS

She said she like my hands
separating a part of me from me.
I was surprised but concealed it,
didn't say anything right then.
I waited until I got back to my room
and then had a closer look at them.
They seemed perfectly reasonable
hands, which could grasp, might claw,
folded up okay, could hold out for
the next world, couldn't scale my arms
like crabs, would remain brownish-white
depending on what sun they're put into,
callouses coming and going with work
or no work. When I saw her again
she held out her hand to mine.
A bird enters the nest to feed
the ten fingers of her babies.

—Steve Lewandowski

## BIG DOG

I bring you
this head,
full of breath—
takingly beautiful
images of yourself

       and put it in
your lap.

Now I breathe
more quietly.

Now you pat me.

Now I sigh.

In a moment or two
I'll get up and
be a man again.

—Anselm Hollo

# MOONLIGHT

I know when the sun is in China
because the night shining other-light
crawls into my bed. She is moon.
Her eyes slit and yellow she is the last
one out of a dingy bar in Alburquerque—
Fourth Street, or from similar avenues
in Hong Kong. Where someone else has also
awakened, the night thrown back and asked,
"Where is the moon, my lover?"
And from here I always answer in my dreaming.
"the last time I saw her was in the arms
of another sky."

—Joy Harjo

# BREATHING LESSONS

Because you refuse to give me
directions for anything except
how to breathe, I try to relax and
breathe exactly the way you
tell me to. Sometimes it works.
It actually does sometimes work.
I breathe in and out sometimes
for an entire afternoon. I imagine
I am the Queen of Spain and
you are the Prime Minister, my
breathing instructor, my interpreter
at The Court of Royal Surprises. How
did you learn to achieve such fluency?

I know a man once who forever
held his breath right in the middle of
significant moments. Without
notice, he would disappear, flatten out,
slip into the mirror, turn himself
inside out, invisible. He never did
acquire the knack of easy breathing.
just in and out, in and out, like a
squeeze box, lungs expanding and
contracting in tune to the music, an
unheard melody, one of those sweet ones.

Today, again, I intend to begin breathing.
Tomorrow I might actually break into song.

—Ansie Baird

# DIFFERENT PLACES TO PRAY

Everywhere, everywhere she wrote; something is falling –
a ring of keys slips out of her pocket into the ravine below;
nickels and dimes and to do lists; duck feathers from a
    gold pillow.
Everywhere someone is losing a favorite sock or a clock
    stops
circling the day; everywhere she goes she follows the ghost
    of her heart;
jettisons everything but the shepherd moon, the hopeless
    cause.
This is the way a life unfolds: decoding messages from
    profiteroles,
the weight of mature plums in late autumn. She'd prefer a
    compass
rose, a star chart, text support messages delivered from the
    net,
even the local pet shop – as long as some god rolls away
    the gloss
and grime of our gutted days, our global positioning
    crimes.
Tell me, where do you go to pray – a river valley, a pastry
    tray?

—Susan Rich

## ANCESTORS
## AT THE SIZZLING SZECHUAN PALACE

The restaurant is crowded, noisy,
Steam clouds flee the kitchen heat
While outside the traffic river honks
Through the chair-propped door.
I bury myself in a cup of coarse tea,
A bowl of plain rice, but when I look up
It all comes clear —
This is the heaven realm of bodhisattvas.
One stands squeezed between chairs
In the aisle and nurses her newborn
Beside the flashing Tsing Tao sign,
Another feeds her daughter fried string beans
With chopsticks one by one. Grandfather
With thick ears is yelling to his wife who leans
Closer, smiling, nodding yes! Yes! Deaf to
Everything he and everyone else has to say,
Boys with large grins tussle over the last spare rib,
Shiny haired girls kick each other under the table
With their spanking new leather shoes.
Wake up! Wake up! They all say.
Keep doing the best you can !
And suddenly a homeless man with a bright
Watermelon patch of skin over half his face
And not a tooth in his mouth rushes in

And scurries from table to table like a whirlwind
That pats the children on their heads and laughs
With his arms around the old folks like friends
At a wedding before chasing himself out the door
And leaving behind a breeze that blows all the way
From the Yangtse at Liang right through the palace
Of human love and cools us with a joy rarely seen,
Pretty soon we settle into the chattering hum again
As Grandmother continues to nod and smile,
But there is a quiet happiness at each table
That wasn't here before, beneath the hum
The sound of Bodhidharma's straw sandals
Can be heard as he steps from his floating leaf
Onto fertile Chinese soil.

—Peter Levitt

# THE OLD WPA SWIMMING POOL
# IN MARTINS FERRY, OHIO

I am almost afraid to write down
This thing. I must have been,
Say, seven years old. That afternoon,
The families of the WPA had come out
To have a good time celebrating
A long gouge in the ground,
That the fierce husbands
Had filled with concrete.

We knew even then the Ohio
River was dying.
Most of the good men who lived along that shore
Wanted to be in love and give good love
To beautiful women, who weren't pretty,
And to small children like me who wondered,
What the hell is this?

When people don't have quite enough to eat
In August, and the river,
That is supposed to be some holiness,
Starts dying,
They swim in the earth. Uncle Sherman,
Uncle Willie, Uncle Emerson, and my father
Helped dig that hole in the ground.

I had seen by that time two or three
Holes in the ground,
And you know what they were.

But this one was not the usual, cheap
Economics, it was not the solitary
Scar on the poor man's face, that respectable
Hole in the ground you used to be able to buy
After you died for seventy-five dollars and
Your wages tached for six months by the Heslop
Brothers.

Brothers, dear God,

No, this hole was filled with water,
And suddenly I flung myself into the water.
All I had on was a jockstrap my brother stole
From a miserable football team.

Oh never mind, Jesus Christ, my father
And my uncles dug a hole in the ground,
No grave for once. It is going to be hard
For you to believe: when I rose from that water,

A little girl who belonged to somebody else,

A face thin and haunted appeared
Over my left shoulder, and whispered, Take care now,
Be patient, and live.

I have loved you all this time,
And didn't even know
I am alive.

—James Wright

# THE SECRET OF LIGHT

I am sitting contented and alone in a little park near the Palazzo Scaligere in Verona, glimpsing the mists of early autumn as they shift and fade among the pines and city battlements on the hills above the river Adige.

The river has recovered from this morning's rainfall. It is now restoring to its shapely body its own secret light, a color of faintly cloudy green and pearl.

Directly in front of my bench, perhaps thirty yards away from me, there is a startling woman. Her hair is black as the inmost secret of light in a perfectly cut diamond, a perilous black, a secret light that must have been studied for many years before the anxious and disciplined craftsman could achieve the necessary balance between courage and skill to stroke the strange stone and take the one chance he would ever have to bring that secret to light.

While I was trying to compose the preceding sentence, the woman rose from her park bench and walked away. I am afraid her secret might never come to light in my lifetime. But my lifetime is not the only one. I will never see her again. I hope she brings some other man's secret face to light, as somebody brought mine. I am startled to discover that I am not afraid. I am free to give a blessing out of my silence into that woman's black hair. I trust her to go on living. I believe in her black hair, her diamond that is still asleep. I would close my eyes to daydream about her.

But those silent companions who watch over me from the insides of my eyelids are too brilliant for me to meet face to face.

The very emptiness of the park bench just in front of mine is what makes me happy. Somewhere else in Verona at just this moment, a woman is sitting or walking or standing still upright. Surely two careful and accurate hands, total strangers to me, measure the invisible idea of the secret vein in her hair. They are waiting patiently until they know what they alone can ever know: that time when her life will pause in mid-flight for a split second. The hands will touch her black hair very gently. A wind off the river Adige will flutter past her. She will turn around, smile a welcome, and place a flawless and fully formed Italian daybreak into the hands.

I don't have any idea what his face will look like. The light still hidden inside his body is no business of mine. I am happy enough to sit in this park alone now. I turn my own face toward the river Adige. A little wind flutters off the water and brushes past me and returns.

It is all right with me to know that my life is only one life. I feel like the light of the river Adige.

By this time, we are both an open secret.

(Verona)

—James Wright

# BIRDFOOT'S GRAMPA

The old man
must have stopped our car
two dozen times to climb out
and gather into his hands
the small toads blinded
by our light and leaping,
live drops of rain.

The rain was falling,
a mist about his white hair
and I kept saying
you can't save them all
accept it, get back in
we've got  places to go.

But, leathery hands full
of wet brown life
knee deep in the summer
roadside grass,
he just smiled and said
they have places to go
too.

—Joseph Bruchac

# CANTICLE

Let others speak
of harps and
heavenly choirs
I've made my decision
to remain here
with the Earth

if the old grey poet
felt he could turn and
live with the animals
why should I be too good
to stay and die with them

and the great road of the Milky Way,
that Sky Trail my Abenaki ancestors
strode to the last Happy Home
does not answer my dreams

I do not believe
we go up to the sky
unless it is
to fall again
with the rain

—Joseph Bruchac

## SEPTEMBER RAIN

The bees are losing weight,
       have stopped making honey
the silence between the crickets' strokes
       is getting wider
the toads are singing more quietly
       or have laid back deeper in the grass.
In the September rain, my ankles ache.
I'm afraid of what this great change will ask,
I believe it is asking for my crickets' legs
       that I make my songs with
& my hands that trace surfaces
       & divine deep springs.
And my losing them will make
       a beautiful sound.

—Bill Pruitt

# MORNING

In the cold room
the other side of the cardboard wall
at five-thirty in the morning
the priest sounds his drum and bells,
chants, coughs, chants.

From under the electric blanket
the undecipherable sutra
of the complete law
only a paper-thickness away
stirs, reassures, lulls.

Birds of dawn are noisy in the garden
invisible past the white paper
pasted on wooden lattices,
but they and the man up in the early morning
fade from the mind in the bed's warmth.

Every morning I am awakened
but before the priest is quiet
fall back to sleep again
meaning to ponder birds and Buddhas
but returned to the phantom world of dreamed emotions.

When I reawake to reality

I slide back all the paper walls,
let warmed daylight into the room,
and say good morning to the priest
now out sweeping a night's fallen leaves from the moss.

—Edith Shiffert

## SONG FOR A BOWL OF SNOW

Buddha flower, precious stem of bloom,
white apple never tasted, fallen fruit,
end this thirst.

Be mountain, be the oceans, breathed-in-air,
be wise, be gentle, fierce, and then be still.
Have the whole

jewel stared at, body being adored,
drinking of water, all there is to bare,
this flower.

—Edith Shiffert

## SMELLING THE BUDDHA

Because the fox circled our house
under a big-faced moon, then rubbed

its hide against the statue, we discussed
omen, fact, and blessing. Because the guidebook

said, "Red foxes spray when mating
in January, check for a skunk-like odor."

Because the mind can rub against anything,
and the stars just hang out above it all

until we are drawn into sleep.
Next day I awoke, the engine of my body cool,

dressed and crossed the icy yard, the Buddha
sitting small in the center facing west.

Dark small weeds made an aura around
his famous lap and a bit of green drooped

beside his right knee. I bent, then sniffed his head,
and the dead garden made me glad. Because I went

to town that day, I saw a man in a leather jacket opened

to the waist, his chest bare. Beside him, a woman

with a black eye. What I smelled was trouble.
Because god is a fox that circles and breathes me

to attention, because what lives at the center
is always surprise, on one day

I saw a Buddha in the dead garden
and a beaten woman on a bad man's arm.

—Genie Zeiger

# WINTER SOLSTICE

This evening I am glad for winter,
for the impersonal darkness
that lays its hand on everything,
for the skillful weight of benediction
on things we have not finished, for
silence, that crosses over
the imperfect folds of our lives
so we can lie down.

Last year I vowed
to always have something to say;
to become the stone, the river,
wind, and leaves flying.
This year I desire only
a place to stand
like any other blade of grass.

—Connie Martin

# IN THE COURTLY MANNER
## OF TWELFTH CENTURY CHINA I TAKE A WALK
## WITHOUT MUSICAL ACCOMPANIMENT

the road is deep with snow
no soft breeze but howling wind
reshapes this winter mountain

walking through the woods I looked
for my friends but found no one
no bird, no fox, no squirrel, no man
tracks either.
I cd. feel my cheeks flaming in the cold.
The trees seemed to be exquisitely colored,
their barks like jeweled curtains barely
shifting. Energized by what

kind of source of light?
A woman in love asks foolish questions
of the world, though not expecting
more than her breath to answer.

—Barbara Moraff

# PLAYGROUNDS OF BEING

Awake at three, snow falling in the dark,
I breathe cold air in, warm air out.
I lived a thousand lives today.
Insomnia sounds like someone twiddling
the radio dial: inter-spliced commercials,
Mahler, rock and roll, female and male
persuasion, argument and song.
Haha! Here I am in a delicate hush
listening instead to the stations
of the self, the substanceless sounds
of my own being obliterating the world.
And what if tonight is the last night,
the grand finale, the nevermore?
I lie here wondering if the yearning
to be awake is a yearning to disappear.
Sometimes I'm afraid of the ever-flowing
river of the work, afraid that to ask
a single question forever is to be a stone.
One of the dogs yips and sighs in sleep,
then settles into breathing that makes
the sound of a hammock longing,
longing, the soft complaints
of wood to rope, rope to wood.
Why can't the mind bear to stay
in the beauties that surround it?

Over and over I lose myself,
invent myself again. I must be
a multitude of lost inventors.
A human being.
Inside me, the snows of sleep
begin to drift, erasing my footprints
and the pawprints of the dogs.
The little engine of thinking sputters
and dies in the great silence.
Some people will say that these words
make a dull clopping. I hope they sound
like horses on the road—plainspoken

—Chase Twichell

# AFTERWORD

## SOME THOUGHTS ON AN IMPURE POETRY

It is worthwhile, at certain hours of the day or night, to look closely at useful objects at rest. Wheels that have crossed long, dusty distances with their enormous loads of crops or ore, sacks from coal, barrels, baskets, the handles and hafts of carpenters' tools. The contact these objects have had with the earth serve as a text for all tormented poets. The worn surfaces of things, the wear that hands give to them, the air, sometimes tragic, sometime pathetic, emanating from these objects lends an attractiveness to the reality of the world that should not be scorned.

In them one sees the confused impurity of the human condition, the massing of things, the use and obsolescence of materials, the mark of a hand, footprints, the abiding presence of the human that permeates all artifacts.

This is the poetry we search for, worn with the work of hands, corroded as if by acids, steeped in sweat and smoke, reeking of urine and smelling of lilies soiled by the diverse trades we live by both inside the law and beyond it.

A poetry impure as the clothing we wear or our bodies, a poetry stained with soup and shame, a poetry full of wrinkles, dreams, observations, prophecies, declarations of love and hate, idylls and beasts, manifestos, doubt, denials, affirmations and taxes.

The sacred canons of the madrigal and the demands of touch, smell, taste, sight, and hearing, the passion for justice and sexual desire, the sound of the sea —accepting and rejecting nothing: the deep penetration into things in the quest of love, a complete poetry soiled by the pigeon's claw, tooth-marked and scarred by ice, etched delicately with our sweat and use. Until the surface of an instrument is worn smooth through constant playing and the hard softness of rubbed wood reveals the pride of the maker. Blossom, wheat kernel and water share a special character, the profuse appeal of the tactile.

We must not overlook melancholy, sentimentality, the perfect impure fruit of a species abandoned by a penchant for pedantry—moonlight, the swan at dusk, all the hackneyed endearments, surely they are the elemental and essential matter of poetry.

He who would shun "bad taste" in things will fall on his face.

—Pablo Neruda
*Translated by Dennis Maloney*

# ABOUT THE EDITOR

Dennis Maloney is the founding editor/publisher of White Pine Press. He is also a poet and translator. His works of translation include *Between the Floating Mist: Poems of Ryokan*, *The House in the Sand* by Pablo Neruda, *The Landscape of Castile* by Antonio Machado and *The Poet and the Sea* by Juan Ramon Jimenez. His most recent volume of poetry is *Just Enough*.

# Acknowledgements

David Budbill "Bugs in a Bowl" from *Moment to Moment* (1999) by permission of Copper Canyon Press, www.coppercanyonpress.com. "Ben" from *Judevine* (1999) by permission of Chelsea Green Press.

Joseph Stroud "Quantum Pearls" and "Lost in Translation" from *Of This World: New and Selected Poems* (2008) by permission of Copper Canyon Press, www.coppercanyonpress.com.

Lew Welch "I Saw Myself" and "Difficulty Along the Way" from *Selected Poems* Copyright 1970, 1976 by Donald Allen, Executor of the Estate of Lew Welch. Reprinted by permission of City Lights Books.

Sherry Robbins "Muladhara: 4" by permission of the author.

Peter Levitt "Ancestors at the Sizzling Szechuan Palace" from *Within Within* (2008) Black Moss Press by permission of the author.

Rick Fields "Petals" from *Fuck You Cancer* by permission of Marcia Fields

Lal Ded "I have seen an educated man starve" and "I might scatter the southern clouds" translated by Andrew Schelling and reprinted with his permission.

Ghalib "Ghazal 127" and "Ghazal 27" translated by Tony Barnstone and Bilal Shaw and are reprinted with their permission.

Rainer Maria Rilke "Archaic Torso of Apollo" and "The Panther" translated by Joe Cadora and reprinted with his permission.

# COMPANIONS FOR THE JOURNEY SERIES

Inspirational work by well-known writers in a small-book format
designed to be carried along on your journey through life.

Volume 22
*Finding the Way Home*
Poems of Awakening and Transformation
Edited by Dennis Maloney
9788-1-935210-12-2    190 PAGES    $16.00

Volume 21
*What Happened Was . . .*
On Writing Personal Essay and Memoir
Genie Zeiger
978-935210-04-7    106 PAGES    $15.00

Volume 20
*Mountain Tasting*
*Haiku and Journals of Santoka Taneda*
Translated by John Stevens
978-1-935210-03-0    200 PAGES    $16.00

Volume 19
*Between the Floating Mist*
*Poems of Ryokan*
Translated by Hide Oshiro and Dennis Maloney
978-1-935210-05-4    90 PAGES    $14.00

Volume 18
*Breaking the Willow*
*Poems of Parting, Exile, Separation and Return*
Translated by David Lunde
978-1-893996-95-3    96 PAGES    $14.00

Volume 17
*The Secret Gardens of Mogador*
A Novel by Alberty Ruy-Sanchéz
Translated by Rhonda Dahl Buchanan
978-1-893996-99-1    240 PAGES    $15.00

Volume 16
*Majestic Nights*
*Love Poems of Bengali Women*
Translated by Carolyne Wright and co-translators
978-1-893996-93-9    108 PAGES    $15.00

Volume 15
*Dropping the Bow*
*Poems from Ancient India*
Translated by Andrew Schelling
978-1-893996-96-0    128 PAGES    $15.00

Volume 14
*White Crane*
*Love Songs of the Sixth Dali Lama*
Translated by Geoffrey R. Waters
1-893996-82-4    86 PAGES    $14.00

Volume I
*Wild Ways: Zen Poems of Ikkyu*
Translated by John Stevens
1-893996-65-4    152 PAGES    $14.00